The Broken Night

Poems

Bruce Arlen Wasserman

Finishing Line Press
Georgetown, Kentucky

The Broken Night

*For Albert Wasserman: Role model.
Trailblazer. Ever-present friend.*

Copyright © 2022 by Bruce Arlen Wasserman
ISBN 978-1-64662-818-6 First Edition
All rights reserved under International and Pan-American Copyright Conventions. No part of this book may be reproduced in any manner whatsoever without written permission from the publisher, except in the case of brief quotations embodied in critical articles and reviews.

ACKNOWLEDGMENTS

All books come to fruition as a composite of behind the scenes efforts. I am grateful for my family—especially Mariem Neuhaus Wasserman for her Yiddishisms and goading, my mother, Dunia Frydman Wasserman, for the serendipity of creative urge, my father, Albert Wasserman, for always lighting the way, and my wife, Beverly Wasserman, for her available ear and unfailing belief in me.

Publisher: Leah Huete de Maines
Editor: Christen Kincaid
Cover Art: Photo by Bruce Arlen Wasserman,
      Rendered by Holly McClelland, Clementine Studios
Author Photo: Bruce Arlen Wasserman
Cover Design: Elizabeth Maines McCleavy

Order online: www.finishinglinepress.com
      also available on amazon.com

Author inquiries and mail orders:
Finishing Line Press
PO Box 1626
Georgetown, Kentucky 40324
USA

Table of Contents

Farmall F-12 1

Porches on Barns 3

A Cow and A Calf and… 5

This Side of Frostbit 7

Elegy of a First Snowfall 8

Today the Sun Shined Black 10

A Loss of Terms 12

The Broken Night 35

Farmall F-12

It was all rusted iron and grinding gears
the 12 in its name standing for 12 horses

though I doubted, at 19 years, I could handle
12 breathing ones, 6 doubletrees and all those

leather-long reins gathered to two hands
at 3 miles-an-hour but the F-12 did 6 when

minted in '36, a year you could still buy rubber
when my father was 15, yet by '43 he was 22

wearing lieutenant's bars and hoping for overseas
though he shipped to Texas and thought to ride

a horse that had a different mind, rearing and
bucking to send him hard-landing like heaped up

khaki-wrinkled laundry, his arm just barely
broken, set straight by an army doctor

like him, a neophyte, a moon-gazed, crazy to go off
to the war every blue-blooded boy wanted

how many frozen nights in his tent under
shell-shocked stars did he dream of endings

how many roaring days at the front lines did machine
guns punctuate his drilling and filling in a canvas

clinic, the lineup of toothaches keeping every dream
from touching blondes, voluptuous bodies wrapped

on bombers, droning keeping any thoughts from home
or family like the fallow of unturned earth

a farmer might plow, every one of his postwar
years spent trying to recapture some memory

he couldn't put a name to, the only certainty
he never saw coming was a son of his riding

some damned old rusty tractor, adding insult to
scavenged medals he kept in his closet, dark symbols

shipped back home when every enemy was vanquished and
bars were put away for good, though somehow they still lived

Porches on Barns

> *The USDA allows… large operations to sell their eggs as organic because officials have interpreted the word "outdoors"*
> —*The Washington Post, "1.6 Million Hens at 3 per Square Foot," Peter Whoriskey, July 13, 2017*

Just to be straight
they're not Amish hens

& they're not hens from
some small kind of family

farm, their henhouse
dirt swarmed with things

like worms & even worse
& they're not backyard hens

foraging the ground for
the catch of the hour

roosters echoing between
house & garden patch

they could catch the avian flu
their wings just bring

problems to the industry
problems that the industry

has figured out already
in leaving off taste for safety

& plastic packs with the
Eggland name, one of ten

are from those 1.6 million
hens, their spaces, "certified,"

three hens per foot, the
new way to lay "outdoors"

& "porches" interchanged with
words like "natural behavior"

& "organic" a substitute for
"propaganda" & "profits."

A Cow and A Calf and…

It was 1974. I was getting by.
I had advanced from goats
—six made-milkers—to a cow,
Elsie. First time heifer. Now
"first time" meant FIRST TIME,
for her and me, not knowing a thing
about how cows deliver,
so when *Elsie* transformed
from just overstuffed to moaning,
mooing, shrieking overstuffed,
I called the neighbor to help.

Now "getting by" meant
no phone, no car, no truck
and "calling" meant
trudging a mile to his farm
and "help" meant my neighbor
telling me what the hell to do

But this… this head-in, tail-out
asswords rotated transfixation
of new calf would never work
and so the neighbor brought
some specialist, sad sack that he was,
his arm all-the-way-to-the-shoulder
in hot, sticky birth canal, all the while
grumbling about the life he couldn't
wait to leave, and struggling to turn
that first calf before birthing stillborn.

While *Elsie*, standing calm,
somehow sensed all that pushing
—five fingers twisting fetus
and wrenching womb—
would eventually work.
And faith, I figured as
not just for farmers
praying for rain, hoping

for healed land and cattle or yield
to pay the banker one more season—

faith, I figured, is far from fact.
It's a heifer,
heaving every load of life,
trusting every drop of blood
to strange hands,
as the moon arranges
shadows on the ground
and things work out
beyond all control.

This Side of Frostbit

It wasn't that I wanted to carry the groceries
three-and-a-half miles through roads thick ribbed
with snowdrifts, when the thermometer's red
said twenty below and the smack-crack reverb
of freezing sap telegraphed it was too cold
to be outside.

It wasn't that I wanted my feet to freeze, first
the toes, then the soles until what felt like clubs
chuffed puffs of snow with every step, because
it took a while for the county to plow beyond that strip
of iced tar I was heading for, winding past stunted trees
and cattle frosted over like Currier and Ives cards.

It's just that I was never prepared for winter at all,
summer's earnings used up by the time leaves fell,
nothing left to stash for a frozen day, but even if I had,
no battery in the world would make the truck's starter
spin in the dead of a Minnesota winter, and gas,
at 49 cents, cost more than a hike so I carried tandem

Packs on my back, stacked, one behind the other to haul
that week's canned beans and corn, flour and oil and wilted
greens, those I could find that far north, and sometimes fruit,
in that hundred pounds of canvas, enough to tip my scrawny
six feet, carving snow angels each week with frozen toes
and nose and mitted fingers just this side of frostbit.

Elegy of a First Snowfall
in memoriam, Robert Steven

I.
These flakes, these slick-sided
packets of wet, the snowy view
out the old brick arch & the
worn whitewash & wavy glass
somehow giving the sense of *my* room
making this long wooden table, *my*
table, same way this moment replays
memories from that last time
—though not the best ones—
even though here I'm far from frozen
& my fingers are pink & flush
& not bloodless-white & reeling from
thawing, right away it all brings back
the day your soul slipped clean
to parts unknown without a chance
to say one word, without a dram of here
& now to drink before gone & done
had vacuumed home your last breath
as a nod to the permanence of vacancy,

II.
voicing vowels of silence that
only imagination can conjugate
& verbs lacking words lacking
lungs to power through any
sentiment, lacking your deadpan
face behind every speck of humor
never knowing one moment
from another minus that glint
in your eye, even that instant
hidden from view like life
behind a mirror: inscrutable
inoperable, lost to everyone
but you & what remains
is tercets of time parsed
into something like memories
& your picture, slow & fading
till every line in your face is

like a well-worn engraving
one thread from torn and
beyond any kind of reach.

Today the Sun Shined Black

The universe tilted a little to the left when I awoke,
horizon where it shouldn't have been
the frozen dirt, bereft of green blades, was covered
in essence of slurpee, flavor missing,
as if some disadvantaged deliverer forgot
life is supposed to be sweet, moments
are meant to be savored in icy delight

Instead, the wind howled gale songs
outside your stall, the hay I left you last night
remained untouched, your appetite
diminished to the point of despair,
your agony, more present
than the dust trying to leave
the frozen ground as you paced, hooves searching

I smoothed your coat, removed
mud clods from yesterday's rolling
in receding snow, brown spheres of a lack
of concentricity, markers of the frivolity
that separates your equine from my human brain,
your recognition of simple pleasure
availed in a moment of horse abandon

How many years have passed since our purpose
was cemented through thin strands of leather,
since it was tied to telegraph keys inlaid with silver
that you carry and balance, your willingness to work
invariably certain, the light in your good eye
reflecting contentment, a poker player's
royal flush unveiled to breathless wonder

You surprised me when you stepped out as if
we had never missed a day of our ranch life
and you no longer suffered with every step,
even though held breath and bulging ribs
betrayed the knife points you had to walk on,
and bobbing of your head traced out random winces
escaped from the façade of relaxed, composed

It was easy to see the sum that our ride cost you—
your hind end slipped as you walked the fence line,
your movements, like stiff finger paints on a paper bag,
no longer do you own refinement, the ballet of your
youth perished somewhere within your string halt,
it drowned in sugarness within any one of your founders,
it died and became irretrievable to your flesh, to your soul

I was surprised at the finish that your body wasn't nervous,
that your spirit breathed uninterrupted beauty
as you followed me, just like you always have, each footfall
leaving one last print in the snow, each pause as casual
as any other day, for assessment of the view, the mountains
you would never see again, the finding of the last few blades of green
before our two souls locked together, my hand on your nose

your ease was more present than mine could ever be,
the tears freezing to my cheek, the sole marker of our end

A Loss of Terms

1: Zeitgeist

Breath

It wasn't easy
being named
after him
the only one
of the covenant
the father
of countless grains of sand
inheritor
of everything:
the earth
the promise

But that was the name they gave you

They must have known
as you swam
inside your lake
what it was, your future
how it would
play beyond
blocks of wood
beyond dirt
that scraped your knees
in Sebastopol
when you fell down
when you bawled
and loosed tears
time taught you to hide

Abraham.
Father of Nations.

Penned with inkpot
and quill
on sheepskin
with steady hand

on even lines
that don't exist
in perfection
that's always chased
but never caught

until released

2: Vergence

At three you had straight hair

Locks like Sir Lancelot's page
with lace collar, the outline
of seriousness
for a three-year-old
all pudgy legs
and plump arms
that had been playing
not frozen in time
on Kodak
paper, stained

But the eyes, the eyes

Perhaps you knew
even before long pants
before higher math
and dissecting a frog
antebellum Menlo Park
and popularity with girls
that your life's work
would tally
that you would be
one of the few
the twenty-three
that made it
the other fifty
conducting cable cars

writing symphonies
of squealing brakes
in San Francisco
where you didn't want
to leave your heart
though you left
singleness
for that blonde
the one, chased
who didn't return calls
for a year
three hundred sixty-five
foggy days alone
working in a tiny
room, the first patient's
recitations not M, i, s, s
as you elevated
i, s, s
as you daydreamed
i, p, p, i when Novocaine
proved
it wasn't designed
for the alcoholics
the elevator operator ran
to your one room
all you could afford
with the leftovers
from Army pay
lucky to be alive
to have missed the bombs
the Germans sent
to blow your tent clinic
to the stars
beyond the dreams
the yellowed photograph
hints at, what we will
never see within

the eyes, the eyes

3: Transphoresis

It was your studiousness

By the time
you were twelve
it set you apart
separated you
from the others
like dominos
of a different color
like nuclei
that found a way
away
from their crowded
platforms, shifted
from basal cells like
weightless astronauts
weighing what is left
watching it float
off the scale, the norm
the measure

You were like that

Always in your own
gravity, somehow
attracting the gathering
of others, leading
not waiting
for a wake-up call
awake and calling
out the future you
were meant to inhabit
the programs, the studies
the future others
would try for
and miss

You were like that

You tried and caught
not catch and release
catch and catch
and catch, climbing
a ladder hand and foot
generations
removed
but still Abraham
his offspring
watching angels
ascend

You were like that

4: Record Details

Properties
unique
to your
systems:

When Israel was in Egypt land
—let my people go

It's hard to imagine
you ever sweated
as a boy
did you run
as fast as you could
when you played
baseball, when you
pretended to be Babe Ruth
with the Yankees, 1927?
When you daydreamed
you saw life
without constant reminder
without kike and jew-boy
closed doors
and lost
opportunities

Oppressed so hard they could not stand
—let my people go

Despite
disadvantage
the folding
of your father's businesses
soup lines
at sixteen
you were already in college
had a vision
saw the future
a way
a life
a new world
like Columbus
a secret code's dispersion
Marrano
in your DNA

Go down, Moses,
way down in Egypt land

The culmination
the realization, the decision

and a changed name

5: Peristalsis

Your father, your household

Was always moving
he was a jack
of all trades
a master
and everything he touched
was made of metal or wood

But you never dreamed that direction

You were sent
to military school
couldn't visualize
wrenches and grease guns
screws and nuts and bolts
as parts of the future
though you worked
odd jobs
the same place your father
riveted, the naval yard
coppersmithing skills
an asset
despite his jewishness

But your hopes didn't live there

Your hands imagined
conjuring something else
career sophistication
in a time when
bread lines
were the recent memory
and college
as foreign as the Yiddish
spoken at home
where you didn't listen
and played your trumpet
and spoke in a jazz diction

Music, music
music, language
well beyond the ink
any paper could hold
your recordings on acetate
the needle
scratching inside your mind, though

not as loud as the sound of your imaginings

6: Onomatopoeia

Lips

Were made
for sips

At eighteen
you drink
your fill
at twenty-two
you enlist
lieutenant
the Army
because
you never liked
ships
your first port is Texas

Your charge, teaching soldiers the tat tat clank
of machine guns, not your first love

In your time off
you are bucked off
from horseback
six months later
your transfer
to Europe
they ship you
across rising falling
seas
a recycled
ocean liner
filled with GIs
a one-way trip
to war scaled bigger
than all the horizons
you'll ever gaze
the creaking boat
sloshing its way

To the front,
to duty:

the teeth of the infantry

7: Morphogenesis

In 1960 you are President

17th District, the photograph
shows you in a straw hat
name tag in the band
like a dealer from Reno
or the Mad Hatter
and success follows
your evolution, follows success
—war now long forgotten—
your face, more seasoned
meat where lean had been
and receding hairline, but
isn't that fitting
for a father of two boys
husbanding a woman
every man's eyes trace?

Peace, peace to him that is far off,
and to him that is near, saith the Lord

You always love routine

Excel at being
defined a workaholic
two and a half decades
before Wayne Oates
dreams of confessing
even the sun catching
a few more minutes
by the time you are out
the door to screen images

on your viewbox, to reread
hand-scribbled notes
before patients begin
appearing at 7 a.m.
like flowers opening
to your presence
in the practice you start
with borrowed cash
after the Army

I have seen his ways, and will heal him:
I will lead him also, and restore comforts

In 1960 your boys are six and eight

You bring the youngest
along to lectures
hoping dentistry
will seep into
his pores
like a well soaked mulch
in your garden
your Bermuda shorts
and bony knees
a mismatched art
so far removed from
the white smock
the shrink-wrapped
identity that said "you"
since the first time
you wore it
your gloveless fingers
immune to blood
and disease since
before you rescued
the mouths of soldiers
hoping to live another day
needing freedom from
tooth pain to bring freedom
to others' pain

the nearly dead
of the concentration camps
yet to be released

*I dwell in the high and holy place, with him also that is
of a contrite and humble spirit, to revive the spirit of the humble*

It is surprising
in the end
how much relies

completely on you

8: Kinesis

When in Rome…

Bell-bottoms
are the uniform of the day
hair is shoulder length
for everyone else
at least your sideburns grow
while every other hair on your head
abandons ship
as if each follicle knows you
could never be hip enough
so why even try?

It's the good life, full of fun, seems to be the ideal

The Seven Dwarves say
to whistle while you work
but you are non-conformist
The Supremes sing
"Stop! In the Name of Love"
while you warble Sinatra
swapping sine waves
in your tiny room
with the sound of the drill

perfuming the air with
your chorus of live performance
diminishing the impact
the smell of burning tooth
your patients love you
and even if they could
tune you out, they wouldn't

Yes, the good life, lest you hide all the sadness you feel

Is it Frank or you?
no one cares, there is something
to be said for happiness in a time
when four protesters are shot
and killed at Kent State
—they were just students—
and the Weathermen
blow themselves up
instead of the military
they intended and
when 14 Army officers
are indicted for the My Lai
Massacre while Apollo 13
shoots toward the moon
and US troops shoot
toward Cambodia
making ever larger war
when you
were in the Army
you saved lives

Yes, the good life, to be free and explore the unknown

Your voice
is always
better
than the tiny radio
crammed in the corner
so you sing and sing
and if you didn't need to stand

perfectly still
while drilling and filling

you might just break out in dance

9: Iontophoresis

There are always two parts

To every problem
but you are a solution
a monolith
others lean on
like a stone in
Stonehenge
reliable
day or night
hot or cold
even blizzards
you are immoveable
though you always
wear gloves in winter
because your fingers
turn blue
as they freeze, you say
becoming useless
and what good is a dentist
without fingers?

Life is a series
of patches, sometimes
held tight with glue
other times with stitches
faint traces, even
a single thread
you are the strand
knitting together
your work, public service
your patients: they celebrate

you, bring their children
their children's children
to Uncle Al
your jokes are worn
like holes in soles
that tickle feet, but
at 59, your boys are grown
you hardly pause
traveling the world collecting
medals—this time earned
without helmet or gun—
a tuxedo, your uniform
formal balls the battlefield
you dance the night away
as hair thins more
but you don't care
you just croon

and bring Sinatra to work

10: Gezai Gesunt

Your mother was strong

She shed opinions, wisdom
Yiddish in fragments
her decorated language
dressed in history
extracted from the clay
of Polish earth, brought over
on the boat
to the New World
the land of opportunity
and a dust bowl
sandwiched
between two world wars
between chickens in the coop
and an old Model T
brushed black

on a day that wasn't windy
parked outside
the screened-in porch
your mother was strong

Men ken nisht tantzen oyf tzvey chasunas oyf eyn mol

You can't dance at two weddings
at one time, she would say

And you are just like her
shared tenacity
and the way it takes forever
to forgive a wrong
but when Poland
abolishes socialism
and Germany reunifies
when Iraq invades
Kuwait and US forces
move closer, when the Royal
New Zealand Navy stops
giving sailors rum
you are sixty-nine
with no grudge important enough
to keep
no pain
worth nursing
like the schnapps
you used to share
with your father
while your mother
watched and disapproved

Fun a bis'l un a bis'l vert a fulehn shis'l

A little and a little adds up
eventually, she would say

And you are nothing like her
you speak no Yiddish

hold no superstitions
don't take whiskey
with honey for a cold
or bring old furniture
into your house
you aren't in the least bit
interested
in living in an apartment
or walking
the circumference
of a park every day
the same route
week by month
by year

Ven der mazal kumt, shtelt im a shtul

When good luck comes
pull up a chair for it, she would say

And you are always lucky
every raffle you enter
every donation
yields stuff
—cameras and wine
tickets and dinners
and vacations—as well
as things nobody wants
they find you
as if you have elastic cords
and magnets, as if you
are a magician
and iron, all in one

Dos lebn iz di gresteh m'tzieh, men krigt es umzist

Life is the greatest bargain
—you get it for free, she would say

You are always lucky

Luck is your outlook
your raison d'être,
the Hubble Telescope
you view all Space through
shuttled in your retirement
as an adjunct to the book
you always carry
—just in case—
you see yourself as lucky
when John Paul II visits Mexico
and you stay home
when Nelson Mandela tours
North America
and you stay home
when Mikhail Gorbachev
flies in and out of Ottawa
in only 29 hours
and you stay home
why become anything
other than calm?
You are retired
you collect
Social Security
check on the mail
every day
eat dinner out
with the wife
other men still want
travel sometimes
or not at all
measure your blood sugar

you are always lucky

11: Elastance

The years tiptoe in

With subdued voice

they mumble
hardly recognizable
speech, the years speak
as if they belong
to someone else
rushing
through the door, screaming
or just crashing
the window, shattering
glass as if existence
doesn't exist
they are never in stasis
there is something about
minutes, hours
days, months, years
their passing
when time talks
it's imbalancing
like standing on the foot
that has fallen asleep

The years tiptoe in

Your 79
a collection
a white remains of hair
and diabetes and swollen knees
and neuropathy, the list
becomes longer
as you become shorter
yin versus yang
in a twelve round
no-holds-barred
fight to the finish
the referee, absent
but you see no problems
take every day's
punches as they come
bending and twisting
like Muhammad Ali

with Joe Frazier
your routine interrupted
by a left to the cheekbone
a right to the jawbone
but you are resilient
resistant to the wear
the pummeling
the decline and the loss
of elasticity
as the years continue

every one, just a little longer

12: Corporeal

Something happens with swelling

When you can't feel
your feet, they can't feel
the gas pedal or the brakes
and metal crumples
and things break
like your Mercedes
the unspoken bounty
of the vanquished
in your mind, your
tour of Germany
when the camps
were being liberated
still fresh within breath
still cringing at the words
"Nazi," "German," "Ghetto"

Your car is war spoil

Sleek, black, war spoil
though when you bought it
the status of ownership
seemed a better reason

now your unfeeling toes
take their revenge, pummel German
fenders with a lack of braking
crush Teutonic
ingenuity
through better smashing
now your feet get to
choose: the victim and
the circumstance
and the pinnacle of German
engineering becomes deformed
in an instant, the subject of mass
ad campaigns destroyed
by the subject of mass
destruction, all wrapped up
in its subliminal package, addressed
to you, care of diabetic neuropathy
and the feet that can no longer sense
even though your sense knows better
your car is war spoil

Something happens when muscles atrophy

As the pain of use becomes
the pain of disuse
as dreams become further
from reality
because it's hard enough
to get out
of your chair
so traveling two hours
has become as inaccessible
as shuttling to the moon
as untenable as a deep sea dive
or climbing Everest or writing
300 pages in 3 days
you try a spring loaded cushion
sounding like something
for someone else, you try
a motorized chair, delivered to

your ever-crowded space
but those don't work
so you acquiesce to the
decline of future
ups and downs, you
struggle to slide along
using a walker, managing
an ever-slowing pace that becomes
your signature dish, your
Chef de Cuisine's monumental
achievement of not cooking
not moving, not improving

Oh, the days of wine and jazz and roses

Beneath a canopy of stars, a balmy
summer night, the type you dreamed of
in Europe in your tent, your assistant
Private Skinner, cranking the drill
faster and slower between the reports
of guns and mortars—at least you never
caught shrapnel as you drilled
and filled, squeaky silver forced into place
your perfectly cobbled patches in the lives
of soldiers, their moments uncertain
as yours now, this final, intact decade
the international year of biodiversity
and youth, combatting poverty
and social exclusion
lucky you weren't in Haiti
the day before your birthday
because the earthquake there
was the seventh deadliest on record
though less destructive
than only one labor camp
and the Germans had so many…
theirs, a quick decline
yours, a slower
cycle of
infections, healing, infections

leg wraps, infections
feet so painful you can't walk
infections, medications
that don't work, infections

and finally: pneumonia, sepsis, kidney failure
a loss of words, a waning consciousness, a lack of breath

13: Apnea

You

Are a deep sea diver
your lifeline:
clear tubing

Oxygen vaporizing
puffs
lost
in a room
filled
with disappearing fables
with stories
of placid waters
floating streams
beyond
the visions
that hover
around your head
children
of imagination
and flesh
holding
your hand
caressing
a pulse
too weak
too hopeful
of seeing

oxygen
starved
breathing
give almost open eyes

Just

one
more
chance.

footnotes:
Peace, peace to him that is far off, and to him that is near, saith the Lord. Isaiah 57:19.
I have seen his ways, and will heal him: I will lead him also, and restore comforts. Isaiah 57:18.
I dwell in the high and holy place, with him also that is of a contrite and humble spirit, to revive the spirit of the humble. Isaiah 57:15

The Broken Night

The air is calmed, unmoved
by my breath, the leaves in repose
as if lungs could no longer fill,
as if a thermal would waft and not
a soul would notice, except the spiral
of flies, recruits, witnesses of the tacking
of ribbon, black ink, to paper
by mechanics too advanced for da Vinci
and buried in archaic heaps, rusting
metal irreparable in this instant.

If I hold a lever, if only
I could, if I could control the spaces
with just the right touch, with a lack
of the wrong key, with a tenderness
splitting time in an echo, ringing bells
and ears without improper punctuation,
without the wrong fingertip driving
movement across the substance of incantation
and silk without even a little missing
letter, if I could do that, would it bring
back the volume of your air so I wouldn't
have to conjure from my memory from my
thoughts from my dreams?

Or would the picture of you still be static,
your breath-points inoperable as my ability
to dream you are still here, answering me.

Bruce Arlen Wasserman assembled his first poetry manuscript with a typewriter on the kitchen table when he was seventeen. "The free verse of that work used rhythm to portray a harsh-edged city contrasted with the soft, lush features of natural elements," he says. As a young man, he farmed and worked as a blacksmith in northern Minnesota, building his own blacksmith shop from the ground up using sawmill slabs and discarded poles. He drove a tractor-trailer in college, edited professional journals, wrote as a freelance journalist and is a dentist. He has been nominated for a *Pushcart Prize*, was a semi-finalist for the *Francine Ringold Awards for New Writers*, a semi-finalist for *The Proverse Prize* and won the *Anna Davidson Rosenberg 2019 Poetry Award*. His fiction manuscript, *The Aroma of Light* was a finalist with LSU Press.

Bruce received an MFA from Vermont College of Fine Arts. He is a literary critic for the *New York Journal of Books* and his writing has been published in the *Proverse Poetry Prize Anthology, The Fredericksburg Literary and Art Review, The River Heron Review, Kindred Literary Magazine, Broad River Review, Cathexis Northwest Press, High Shelf Literary Magazine, Wild Roof Journal* and *Washington Independent Review of Books*. He has produced poetry shows to raise funds for nonprofits in Colorado and Wyoming. Beyond writing, Bruce creates visual art as a potter at Bruce Arlen Wasserman Studio, where he draws from a reservoir of poetry and his experience in working iron and wood, correlating a continued exploration of language, function and esoteric form. At other times he is a musician, trains horses, conserves the earth on his little ranch in Colorado and still drives a truck.